SCIENCE Q&A
WEATHER
— Janice Parker —

Weigl Publishers Inc.

Published by Weigl Publishers Inc.
350 5th Avenue, Suite 3304, PMB 6G
New York, NY 10118-0069

Website: www.weigl.com

All of the Internet URLs given in the book were valid at the time of publication. However, due to the dynamic nature of the Internet, some addresses may have changed, or sites may have ceased to exist since publication. While the author and publisher regret any inconvenience this may cause readers, no responsibility for any such changes can be accepted by either the author or the publisher.

Library of Congress Cataloging-in-Publication Data

Parker, Janice.
  Weather : Science Q & A / Janice Parker.
     p. cm.
  Includes index.
  ISBN 978-1-59036-952-4 (hard cover : alk. paper) -- ISBN 978-1-59036-953-1 (soft cover : alk. paper)
  1. Weather--Juvenile literature. I. Title.
  QC981.3.P367 2009
  551.5--dc22
                              2008003891

Printed in China
1 2 3 4 5 6 7 8 9 0   12 11 10 09 08

Project Coordinator
Heather Hudak

Design
Terry Paulhus

Photo credits

All images provided by Getty Images unless otherwise noted.

Yankee Publishing, Inc: page 7 bottom.

CONTENTS

What is weather?

Have you ever seen a tornado, had a sunburn, or watched your dog hide from a thunderclap? If so, you have experienced just three of the thousands of effects the weather can have on your life. Weather is caused by the conditions that exist in the air around you. It can be hot, cold, wet, or dry. It can be windy, calm, stormy, or **humid**.

All weather has four main ingredients. These are temperature, wind, water, and air pressure. We know a great deal about the science at work in making weather, but not enough to make weather predictable. Weather can change without warning. It can sometimes work silently, such as when the Sun's rays burn your skin, or it can make a grand entrance, as tornadoes and hurricanes do, leaving destruction in its path.

How did people forecast weather in the past?

For centuries, people have tried to learn about and forecast the weather. Throughout the world and throughout history, people have used many different methods of predicting the weather.

find it quick

Visit **http://teacher.scholastic.com/ activities/wwatch** to learn more about forecasting the weather.

Hundreds of years ago, people in Europe believed that animal behavior changed depending on the weather. For example, people believed that hedgehogs could predict the end of winter.

When European settlers arrived in North America, they could not find hedgehogs, so they decided to use groundhogs instead.

According to tradition, groundhogs end their hibernation on February 2nd, signaling the end of winter. The tradition says that if a groundhog comes out of the ground and sees its shadow, it gets frightened and runs back into the ground. This means there will be six more weeks of winter. Scientists who have studied the groundhog theory have concluded that this traditional method of forecasting weather does not work.

■ Punxsutawney Phil is a well-known weather-predicting groundhog.

A tradition that has a history of success is the Old Farmer's Almanac. First published in 1792, the Old Farmer's Almanac gives information about weather, the rise and set of the Sun, and the tides. Its weather forecasts are correct about 80 percent of the time—a very good rate. The forecasts are given on the basis of weather folklore and a secret scientific formula. Many farmers and other people whose jobs depend on the weather rely on the advice in the Old Farmer's Almanac.

I spy

The Old Farmer's Almanac is so accurate that the United States government almost prevented it from being published during World War II. In 1942, a German spy was caught by officials on Long Island, New York. The spy had a copy of the Old Farmer's Almanac in his pocket. The government was worried that the publication could supply the enemy with important information. In the end, it was decided that the almanac could continue to be published.

How is temperature measured?

Everyone can tell the difference between hot and cold. Often, however, it is important to know exactly how hot or how cold something is.

Temperature is measured by thermometers. Scientists in the 17th century realized that water always boils and freezes at the same temperatures. This discovery helped scientists make a temperature scale. The scale allowed all scientists to measure temperature with the same numbers.

The German scientist, Gabriel Fahrenheit, was the first person to use mercury in thermometers. Mercury responds quickly to temperature changes, swelling when it gets warmer and shrinking when it gets colder. Fahrenheit made a temperature scale that is still used today in the United States. He set 0° Fahrenheit as the lowest winter temperature where he lived in Germany.

In 1742, Anders Celsius, a Swedish astronomer, developed a scale with simpler numbers. He made the freezing point of water 0°C and the boiling point 100°C. His system is used today, especially by scientists, who find the system easier to use than the Fahrenheit method. Most countries in the world have also adopted the Celsius system. The United States is one of the only countries still using the Fahrenheit system.

■ Mercury, also known as quicksilver, can be very dangerous to human health. Most thermometers today use other substances to measure temperature.

Revolution

Galileo Galilei is credited with inventing the thermometer in the 1590s. Galileo also built the first effective telescope and used it to prove that Earth revolves around the Sun.

What is the Sun?

The Sun rises and sets everyday. It is always sunny somewhere on Earth. The Sun gives us warmth and light. What else does the Sun do for Earth?

■ The Sun is about 4.5 billion years old. Scientists believe there has been life on Earth for about 3.5 billion years.

The Sun is the key to life on Earth. Without the Sun, the planet would freeze, and all life that relies on its energy for growth and food would die. People who lived in ancient times worshiped the Sun. They knew of its great importance in maintaining life on Earth. However, they did not understand the science behind the Sun's power. We now understand some of the ways the Sun's energy influences weather. Everything from wind to temperature is affected by the Sun.

The Sun is a giant ball of fiery gases 93 million miles (150 million kilometers) away from Earth. It is our closest star and one of the hundred billion stars in our galaxy.

The Sun sends out large amounts of energy in all directions. Only about two-billionths of the total output reach Earth. This is enough energy to provide plenty of light and heat for all the plants and animals on Earth. Without the Sun's energy, the temperature on Earth would be no higher than -418° Fahrenheit (-250° Celsius).

The Sun's energy arrives on Earth as different types of radiant energy, or rays. Although you cannot see **infrared** rays, you can feel them. When infrared rays hit your skin, or any other object, the energy usually turns into heat. Nearly all of the heat on Earth comes from the infrared rays of sunshine.

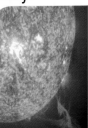

Hot enough for you?

The temperature on the surface of the Sun is 10.832° Fahrenheit (6,000°C). The Sun's core reaches a temperature of about 27,000,000°F (15,000,000°C).

What happens when sunlight reaches Earth?

When the Sun's rays reach Earth, the energy may be absorbed by land, water, or air. In each case, the results are quite different.

find it quick

Visit **www.phy6.org/stargaze/ Sun1lite.htm** to learn more about how the Sun affects Earth.

Air absorbs some of the Sun's energy as the rays pass through, but most of the rays move through the air until they reach water or land.

Land features such as soil, rocks, and pavement become warm when they absorb the Sun's energy. As the temperature of the land rises, some of the heat is given off into the air close to the ground. This makes the

■ Water vapor that remains close to the ground is called mist.

air temperature rise. Then, when the air moves, it carries the heat from one place to another.

When water absorbs sunrays, the energy causes some of the water to evaporate, or turn into gas, and enter the air as water vapor. This creates humidity and clouds.

Warm waters

Water can absorb a great deal of heat without showing much of an increase in temperature. Land that is near oceans and large lakes does not become as warm as land that is far from bodies of water. However, water also holds onto its heat energy longer than land does. For this reason, coastal cities stay warmer in the winter than inland cities.

Why do the seasons change?

Everyone on Earth experiences changing seasons. In some places, the difference between winter and summer can be drastic, from sunshine and hot temperatures to snow and ice. Other places experience less noticeable changes, perhaps only a few degrees.

find it quick

More about Earth's seasons can be found at **www.bbc.co.uk/science/space/solar system/earth/solsticescience.shtml**.

Seasons are caused when different amounts of the Sun's energy reach Earth at different times of the year. Earth's **axis** is tilted as it makes its yearlong **orbit** around the Sun. When it is summer in the Northern Hemisphere, the Sun's rays strike the top half of Earth directly.

At the same time, the rays reaching the Southern Hemisphere are more indirect. They cover a much larger area, so the region is cooler. During the spring and autumn, the Sun is most direct at the **equator**.

Here is your challenge!

Create a model of the Sun as it would be seen from space. Use this model to track how the Sun moves across the sky in one 24-hour period.

1. Draw an "X" in the center of a sheet of white paper. Then, place the paper on a flat surface outdoors. Be sure that the paper is in a place where there is sunlight for the entire day.
2. Place a clear plastic bowl upside down over the "X" on the piece of paper. Next, mark the bottom of the bowl with an "X." Be sure the "X" on the paper is in line with the "X" on the bowl. Now, use a pencil to trace the outer edge of the bowl onto the paper.
3. Use a compass to locate north, and mark this spot on the paper.
4. Every hour, place the pencil on the outside of the bowl so that the shadow of the point lines up with the "X" on the paper. Mark the location with a small circle, and label it with the time of day. Repeat this step for several hours.

Can you predict where the next small circle will be placed? Which direction is the Sun moving?

What is the greenhouse effect?

The "greenhouse effect" is the popular term for how the atmosphere helps warm the global **ecosystem**. Just as glass on a greenhouse holds the Sun's warmth inside, so the atmosphere traps heat near Earth's surface and keeps Earth warm. The greenhouse effect makes Earth a good planet for living things.

find it quick

For more information about climate change and global warming, surf to **www.epa.gov/climatechange/kids**.

■ Air travel is a leading cause of the greenhouse effect. Many people who travel on airplanes today donate money to environmental causes to offset their impact on the environment.

As a natural part of Earth's greenhouse effect, the planet periodically warms and cools. Some people are concerned about the present warming trend because it is happening faster than ever before. Many human activities are adding greenhouse gases such as carbon dioxide and methane to the atmosphere. Activities that produce these gases include farming, mining coal, and flying airplanes.

We cannot be sure how global warming will affect us in the future. If greenhouse gases in the atmosphere increase, global temperatures might rise to a level that could become very dangerous. If Earth's water warms and expands, polar ice and **glaciers** may melt. Some coastal areas may be permanently flooded, and people could lose their homes. Changing temperatures could also affect crop growth, causing food shortages in some areas.

Slow down

The average car gives off more than its own weight in carbon dioxide each year. Driving fast burns more fuel and causes more pollution than driving slowly for the same distance.

When are the Sun's rays deadly?

Some of the Sun's energy is necessary for life, but too much can be harmful.

find it quick

To learn how to stay safe from the Sun's harmful rays, check out **www.sunsafetyforkids.org**.

Ultraviolet (UV) rays from the Sun can cause skin cancer, including the deadly form known as melanoma. Other effects of UV rays include damaged eyesight and, possibly, weaker defenses against infection. The United States has estimated that every one percent of **ozone** loss causes thousands more cases of skin cancer each year, and blindness in 100,000 people worldwide. Ultraviolet radiation also harms water animals such as plankton, shellfish, and fish. Too much UV sunlight has caused sheep to go blind in southern Chile. Some frog species could be at risk of **extinction** because UV rays damage their eggs. Crops grow smaller leaves if UV rays increase. This harms food production.

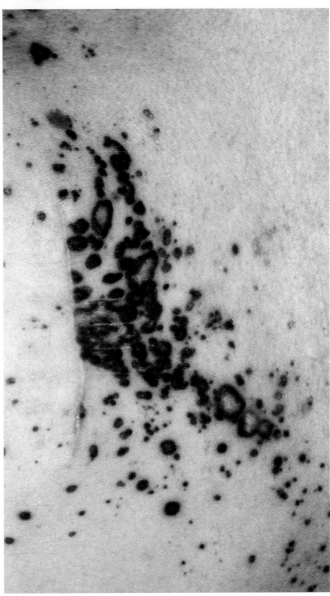

■ Metastatic is a rare type of skin cancer, but it causes most skin cancer deaths.

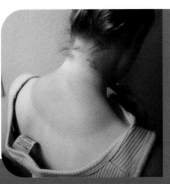

Sun is shining

Sunburns and suntans are caused by two different types of UV rays. A sunburn may become lighter as it heals, but it will never become a suntan.

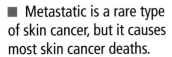

What makes the wind blow?

Wind is the movement of air. Sometimes, air moves so fast that it knocks over buildings. On a very calm day, it might feel like there is no wind at all.

find it quick

Explore **www.weatherwiz kids.com/wind1.htm** to learn more about the wind.

Earth is surrounded by a blanket of air called the atmosphere. The atmosphere is about 186 miles (300 km) thick. This may seem very thick, but compared to Earth's size, the atmosphere is like the skin on an apple. The atmosphere gets thinner on its outer edges. This means there are fewer particles of air higher in the atmosphere than there are closer to Earth's surface.

The wind blows for the same reason that hot-air balloons rise. Air moves, and heat goes up.

Ground that is warmed by the Sun transfers heat to the air. Air molecules move faster when they are heated, bumping into each other more forcefully. The energetic molecules push one another apart, and the air becomes thinner and lighter.

Air will always move from areas where there are many air molecules to areas where there are few. The light air rises like a bubble. At the same time, heavier, cooler air moves in below to take its place. This causes the air to circulate. The basic rule is that whenever warm air and cool air meet, the wind will blow.

DAY

Warm air rises from the land.

Cool air moves in to take its place.

NIGHT

Cool air moves in to take its place.

Warm air rises from the ocean.

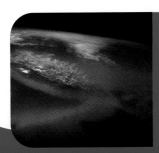

Dust in the wind

Scientists have found that wind can carry dust to North America from places as far away as Africa and China.

How is wind measured?

Much like measuring temperature, the measurement of wind speed and direction is very important. Farmers, pilots, and architects all need to know wind patterns and speeds in order to do their jobs.

Wind vanes, also called weather vanes, are used to tell wind direction. As wind hits the side of a weather vane, the vane is pushed around so that it points into the wind. Airports often use wind socks made of cloth to show wind direction and speed. The socks fill with air and point in the direction the wind is blowing. Today's weather forecasters measure wind speed with an instrument called an anemometer. Most anemometers have several cups that spin when the wind blows. The anemometer counts how often the cups spin around the center. This number tells forecasters how fast the wind is blowing.

You can tell how fast wind is blowing even without instruments. By observing the movements of flags, people, trees, and other objects outside, it is easy to see the difference between a strong wind and a light wind.

■ Weather forecasters use anemometers to measure both wind speed and wind pressure.

Here is your challenge!

Which way is the wind blowing where you live? Make your own weather vane to find out.

1. Stick a pencil in a large lump of clay with the eraser end up. Be sure the pencil is steady.
2. Stick an arrowhead and tail made from cardboard in each end of a drinking straw.
3. Pin the straw onto the eraser.
4. Mark North, South, East, and West on the clay, and use a compass to position the wind vane on the wall of a fence.
5. Watch the vane turn in the wind. In which direction is the wind blowing?

What are air currents?

Wind blows around the world in set patterns. There are many elements that affect the way wind blows.

Imagine Earth is a big, smooth ball of soil, with no water or mountains. Now imagine that it stops rotating. If Earth were like this, the land at the equator would get the most heat, and air currents would always be the same. The heated air would rise and pull cooler air from both the north and south. When air rises, it expands because the pressure is lower at higher altitudes. Expanding air cools. The cooling air above ground would flow both north and south from the equator, then sink down, pushing the air below toward the equator. Air would form regular loops from the equator to the poles. Wind would always blow north and south from the poles to the equator.

Earth's rotation disturbs these ideal patterns. The air sinks to the surface before reaching the poles, causing trade winds to blow. The same thing happens when cold air moves from the poles. More than one "loop" of air helps make the world's air currents. Lakes, oceans, prairies, and mountains also disturb the smooth flow of air.

Polar easterlies
Polar front
Prevailing westerlies
Horse latitudes
Northeast trade winds
Doldrums
Southeast trade winds
Horse latitudes
Prevailing westerlies
Polar front
Polar easterlies

We shall prevail

In some areas, winds follow a regular pattern. The direction the wind blows from most often is called the "prevailing wind." These winds can deform the growth of trees.

What turns wind into a twister?

Tornadoes can happen during severe thunderstorms. Only one thunderstorm in 1,000 produces a tornado. Winds in a tornado can reach 150 to 200 miles (240 to 320 km) per hour.

■ Tornadoes can appear in many shapes and sizes. However, most appear in the form of a funnel.

Many tornadoes never touch the ground, but those that do suck up dirt, debris, and other objects. Tornadoes can even lift cars off the ground and completely destroy houses and other buildings. Roughly 1,000 tornadoes occur in North America every year.

Wild winds form inside thunderclouds as warm air moves in below cool air that is moving in a different direction.

Winds higher up in the cloud blow faster and in a different direction than winds below. The air begins to spin. As the air spins faster and faster, it becomes a column.

The funnel of spinning air pushes down through the cloud toward the ground. This is how a tornado forms.

Dark alley

The states of Texas, Kansas, Oklahoma, Nebraska, and Missouri are known as "Tornado Alley." These states have more tornadoes than anywhere else on Earth—more than 700 each year.

What is El Niño?

Natural disasters can be caused by events happening both inside and around our planet. One event has been blamed for many different disasters all over the world.

find it quick

Learn more about El Niño by finding it in the Weather Encyclopedia at **www.theweather channelkids.com/weatherED**.

Early Spanish sailors noticed periodic changes in water temperatures where they fished off the west coast of South America. They called the rise in temperature El Niño, meaning "Christ Child," because it always happened just after Christmas. The change happened about once every seven years.

Peru's cool coastal waters normally have some of the best fishing areas in the world. During El Niño, however, a change in wind patterns causes the water to warm. The ocean currents change, and the best fishing waters surface far from shore.

■ Landslides and other changes caused by El Niño cause thousands of deaths and billion of dollars in damage.

The shifting patterns of El Niño have many other effects. There are changes in temperature and wind patterns around the world. El Niño has been blamed for everything from droughts in Africa and Australia, to floods in Ecuador, and landslides in California. Some people believe it has even caused outbreaks of tropical diseases.

Look on the bright side

El Niño is not all bad. Researchers have found that El Niño reduces the number of hurricanes developing in the Atlantic Ocean and the number of tornadoes in the central United States.

How does water affect the weather?

Without water, there would be no weather. Water vapor in the air interacts with heat from the Sun to create weather patterns on Earth.

■ Dew forms when surfaces near the ground become cool enough for water vapor in the air to condense. When warm, moist air reaches the temperature at which it cannot hold water in a gas form, beads of water appear on the surface.

Weather only happens in the region of the atmosphere that is about 6 miles (10 km) above Earth. This region is called the troposphere. Only the troposphere contains water that has been evaporated from Earth's surface.

Water vapor is invisible, but even on a bright, clear, cloudless day, there is water vapor in the air. When the Sun shines on oceans, lakes, rivers, and ponds, it always causes some water to evaporate. Evaporation means that water turns from a liquid that people can see into a gas that cannot be seen.

There is a limit to the amount of water vapor that the air can hold. If you try to add more, some of the vapor will condense, or turn into liquid. The temperature of the air determines how much water it can hold. Warm air holds much more water than cold air. For example, air at 86° Fahrenheit (30°C) can hold more than six times as much water vapor as air at 32° Fahrenheit (0°C).

Vaporized

The air in your lungs holds as much water vapor as possible. The water vapor is the same temperature as your body—98.6° Fahrenheit (37°C). When you breathe out in the winter, the warm air from your body combines with cold air that cannot hold as much water vapor. When you "see" your breath, some of the water vapor has condensed into tiny droplets of water.

How do clouds form?

Clouds can be big and fluffy or thin and wispy. They can make rain or offer shade. They can take many different shapes. How are clouds made?

find it quick

Find out more about clouds at
www.weatherwizkids.com/cloud.htm.

■ People can predict the weather based on the type of cloud they see.

Clouds are made of tiny droplets of water or ice crystals in the air. When warm, moist air meets cooler air, some warm air cools and cannot hold all of its water vapor. Some of the extra water changes into a liquid or even freezes. This forms clouds.

Clouds come in a variety of sizes and shapes. Most clouds belong to one of three basic categories—cumulus, stratus, or cirrus. You may also see the word "nimbus" added to a cloud name. For example, a cumulonimbus cloud is a rain cloud.

Cumulus clouds are puffy with flat bottoms. These clouds can be as high as 14,000 feet (4,267 meters) in the air. Cumulus clouds often form on warm summer days and then disappear at night.

Cirrus clouds are made of ice crystals. They form very high in the sky, usually above 25,000 feet (7,620 m). Cirrus clouds have a wispy, feathery appearance. The winds blow cirrus clouds into fine strands that are sometimes called "mares' tails."

Stratus clouds form quite low and often cover the sky like a gray sheet. The clouds barely move, and the air under them is very still. These conditions can make the sky look dull and heavy.

Get cirrus

Airplanes make cirrus clouds when water vapor from their engines forms ice crystals. The clouds look like long streaks high in the sky.

What causes rain?

We know that clouds are made of water, so why are not all clouds rain clouds?

A cloud droplet has a million times less water than a typical raindrop. Cloud droplets are very light and tiny. Stormy air in the sky tosses small droplets around so much that they usually cannot fall to the ground. They will not fall until they collide with each other and join together to make larger, heavier droplets.

If the air is very still, smaller drops may fall to the ground as the form of rain called drizzle. Larger raindrops usually start as ice crystals near the center of cumulus clouds. The ice crystals collect water from droplets in the clouds. The crystals grow larger and larger until they are heavy enough to fall through the

■ Drops of water more than 0.02 inches (0.05 centimeters) in size are rain. Smaller drops are called drizzle.

turbulent air. While passing through warm air close to Earth, the crystals melt and turn into raindrops. If the air temperature remains cold, the ice crystals do not melt. They fall as snow.

During a severe storm, air currents may push upward so violently that they carry growing ice crystals and pellets high into the clouds. Water continues to condense on the crystals until they grow very large. When the ice balls finally fall through the warmer air below, they are too big to completely melt. They fall as hailstones.

Drops of rain

Raindrops are shaped like disks, not teardrops. Raindrops are round when they leave the clouds, but the wind resistance, or pressure, on the way to Earth flattens them slightly.

What is a thunderstorm?

A thunderstorm has very violent winds, thunder, and lightning. Clouds may rise as high as 14 miles (22 km). The energy of a thunderstorm is much greater than the energy of an atomic bomb.

find it quick

Try controlling the weather in a virtual environment at **www.scholastic.com/kids/weather**.

■ Mountain ranges can create interesting weather patterns. Often, one side of a mountain range will experience wet, rainy weather, while the other side will experience dry conditions.

Thunderstorms often occur after a long period of hot weather. This is because the ground becomes very warm from the heat of the Sun.

A thunderstorm begins when drafts of warm air move upward, creating a large cumulus cloud. When the cloud is high enough for the rain to begin, the thunderstorm is mature. As rain falls through the cloud, it cools the air, causing **downdrafts**. The air in the cloud becomes very turbulent. Finally, the rain cools all of the air in the cloud until there are no more **updrafts**. The rain stops, and winds scatter the cloud.

Look up...look way up

You can tell whether a thunderstorm or just rain is coming by looking at clouds in the distance. Tall clouds mean a thunderstorm is on the way. Thinner clouds will bring a slower and steadier rain.

What causes lightning and thunder?

Thunder and lightning can be dangerous, frightening, or beautiful. Something special must happen in the sky to create so much energy.

Ice particles and raindrops in clouds are made of molecules. Collisions between ice particles and raindrops break negatively charged particles, called electrons, off their molecules. When a particle loses electrons, it becomes positively charged. These positively charged particles cause nearby particles to become negatively charged. Positive charges collect in the top part of the thundercloud, while clusters of negative charges collect at the bottom. The ground becomes charged as well. Opposite charges attract each other with such a strong force that the charges leap from cloud to cloud or between clouds and the ground. This giant electric spark is lightning.

When lightning strikes, it instantly heats the air. The quick expansion of the warm air starts a shock wave that is heard as thunder. Lightning and thunder happen at the same time, but thunder is heard later because light travels faster than sound.

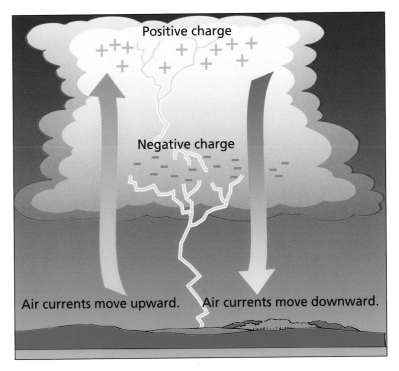

Positive charge

Negative charge

Air currents move upward.   Air currents move downward.

Here is your challenge!

Step 1. Tear a sheet of paper into small pieces, like confetti.
Step 2. Hold a comb close to the bits of paper.
Step 3. Run the comb through your hair.
Step 4. Repeat step 2.

You have created static electricity. This is the same type of electricity as a lightning bolt.

What causes a hurricane?

A hurricane is a powerful storm that can destroy entire cities with wind and rain. A storm can officially be called a hurricane when its wind speed reaches 75 miles (121 km) per hour. Hurricanes cause billions of dollars in damage and kill thousands of people every year.

find it quick

Visit **http://eo.ucar.edu/webweather** to learn how hurricanes form and other interesting weather facts.

A hurricane happens when air currents near the equator begin to circulate, and several thunderstorms are pulled together. Updrafts of warm, moist air form storm clouds, and the rain begins. The condensation of the water releases energy to strengthen the updrafts. At the top, the air moves out and begins to drop. Near the surface of the ocean, the air is drawn back toward the center. The air picks up more moisture from the warm ocean and creates more updrafts. The cycle continues, and the storm grows.

■ Hurricanes cause huge, powerful waves to crash into the shore. This causes the shoreline to be washed away, or eroded. Erosion can cause entire buildings to collapse into the ocean, because the ground below the buildings is washed away.

As long as the hurricane is over water, it can maintain or increase its strength. When it moves onto land, it causes enormous damage to lives and to property in its path. When it runs out of water, the hurricane loses energy and dies out.

Thundering typhoons

Hurricanes only originate in the Atlantic Ocean. Powerful storms that originate in the Pacific Ocean are called typhoons.

Why is fresh water important?

Earth is often called the "water planet" because about 70 percent of its surface is covered with water. However, less than three percent of all the world's water is fresh, drinkable, and accessible.

With such a limited supply of fresh water, a weather disaster such as a drought can cause serious problems. For example, the Mississippi River is the United States' most important inland route for transporting products by boat. Inland barges and tugboats carry their cargoes more than 1,800 miles (2,900 km) south to the Gulf of Mexico. In 1988, a severe drought dried up so much of the river that boat traffic had to stop.

In desperation, the state of Illinois decided it could increase the amount of water in the river by draining water from Lake Michigan and Lake Huron, two of the five Great Lakes. These lakes contain almost one-fifth of the entire world's fresh water. Other states that border Lake Michigan and Lake Huron objected to the plan, and so did the government of Canada. In the end, the drainage plan was abandoned.

■ Droughts can cause many problems for people in affected regions. Along with water shortages, these include death of livestock, fewer crops, wildfires, and desertification. Desertification is when an area becomes so dry it turns into a desert.

Stay fresh

The United States uses about 346 billion gallons (1.3 trillion liters) of fresh water every day.

Weather Careers

Meteorologist

Meteorologists use technology such as computers, **satellites**, and **radar** to help them forecast the weather. They tell people what the day-to-day weather is and what can be expected for the next few months. They also warn people about dangerous weather systems, such as tornadoes and hurricanes.

Meteorologists research ways to prevent weather that is dangerous to humans. This includes **seeding** clouds before they become violent storms. Most meteorologists work in government offices and have degrees in meteorology.

Storm Chaser

Some people try to get as close as possible to tornadoes. These "tornado hunters" or "storm chasers" are well trained in tornado safety.

Storm chasers listen to weather reports for clues about where a tornado might happen. If a tornado appears, the storm chasers have special equipment that will help them observe the storm. Video cameras record the tornado, while other machines measure the temperature, wind speed, and air pressure inside the tornado. The information they collect is given to scientists who study tornadoes.

find it
quick

To learn about other weather careers, visit **www.mscd.edu/~career/meteor.htm**.

Young scientists at work
Test Your Knowledge

Test your weather knowledge with these questions and activities. You can probably answer the questions using only this book, your own experiences, and your common sense.

Fact:

Coastal areas have warmer summers and milder winters than inland areas.

Test:

You can do an experiment to show how water affects temperature. Place an empty glass and a glass full of water in the refrigerator. Wait 15 minutes. Then take the glasses out of the refrigerator. Which glass feels warmer? Look back to page 13 to find out why.

Fact:

One of the best ways to measure wind speed is by observing the effects of wind. Admiral Francis Beaufort designed a wind scale in the 1800s to help sailors judge wind speed. Today's Beaufort scale has been adapted for use on land.

Test:

Match the pictures to the appropriate wind speeds from the Beaufort scale.

A. less than 1 mph (1.6 kph)
B. 8–12 mph (13–19 kph)
C. 25–31 mph (40–50 kph)

D. 47–54 mph (76–87 kph)
E. more than 75 mph (121 kph)

1

2

3

4

5

Answers: 1. C, 2. B, 3. A, 4. D, 5. E

Take a weather survey

Are you prepared for a weather emergency? The American Red Cross and The Weather Channel conducted a survey of 2,039 Americans, aged 18 or older. They were asked a variety of questions to find out how prepared people are in case of a weather-related disaster, such as a flood, blizzard, hurricane, or tornado.

Do you believe that a weather-related disaster like a flood or hurricane could happen where you live?

Would you and your family be prepared if a weather emergency happened right now?

Have you and your family prepared an emergency supply kit to get you through a weather disaster?

Have you and your family ever practiced what to do in case of an emergency?

Would you know what to do and where to go if you were told to evacuate your home?

Do you or any family members have first-aid training?

Survey Results: Nearly every day, reporters and news broadcasters cover stories about weather-related disasters such as droughts, heat waves, cold snaps, tornadoes, and floods. More than half of the people surveyed believed that a weather-related disaster was unlikely to happen where they live. Only one in six people believed such an event was very likely to happen. Only one in seven people said they would be completely prepared if a weather emergency were to happen right now.

Fast Facts

In the eastern Sahara Desert, the Sun shines for 97 percent of possible daylight hours.

Nearly 1,000 square miles (2,590 sq km) of land in China are turning to desert each year. Drought is one of the causes of this disaster, along with erosion and overgrazing by cattle.

The hottest temperature ever recorded on Earth was at Al`Aziziyah, Libya, in 1922. It reached 136.4° Fahrenheit (58°C).

The coldest temperature ever recorded on Earth was at Vostok, Antarctica. On July 21st, 1983, it reached -126.9° Fahrenheit (-88.3°C).

Some areas of the Atacama Desert, in Chile, have not had rain for more than 400 years.

Hurricanes have a center known as the "eye." The storm is shaped like a doughnut, with a calm hole in the middle. During a hurricane, the eye can become full of birds flying to keep out of the storm.

The windiest place on Earth is Commonwealth Bay, on the coast of Antarctica. Winds there can reach speeds of 200 miles per hour (320 kph).

In the Northern Hemisphere, tornadoes spin in a counter-clockwise direction. In the Southern Hemisphere, they spin in a clockwise direction.

The largest snowflake ever recorded measured 15 inches (38 cm) across.

Hail can hit the ground at 80 miles per hour (130 kph).

Glossary

axis: the imaginary line on which Earth rotates

downdrafts: downward moving air in a thunderstorm

ecosystem: a system formed by a community of organisms

equator: an imaginary line around Earth halfway between the poles

extinction: no longer existing on Earth

glaciers: a slow-moving mass of ice

humid: water vapor in the air

infrared: invisible rays from the Sun that people feel as heat

orbit: the curved path of a planet, moon, or satellite around another body

ozone: a layer in the atmosphere protecting Earth from the Sun's harmful rays

radar: a system for determining the speed, distance, or direction of an object

satellites: machines that orbit Earth or other objects in space

seeding: adding substances to clouds in order to make rain fall

turbulent: a disturbance in the flow of air or water

ultraviolet: harmful rays from the Sun

updrafts: upward moving air in a thunderstorm

Index